Oracle of Mystical Moments

By Catrin Welz-Stein

Copyright © 2017 U.S. Games Systems, Inc.

All rights reserved. The illustrations, cover design, and contents are protected by copyright. No part of this booklet may be reproduced in any form without permission in writing from the publisher, except by a reviewer who wishes to quote brief passages in connection with a review written for inclusion in a magazine, newspaper or website.

First Edition

10 9 8 7

Made in China

Published by
U.S. GAMES SYSTEMS, INC.
179 Ludlow Street • Stamford, CT 06902 USA
www.usgamesinc.com

INTRODUCTION

Thank you, dear friend, for choosing the *Oracle of Mystical Moments* and taking it home with you. I hope it will enrich your everyday life. These 52 cards tell all kinds of stories about feminine wisdom, nature and life. For each one, you will find my interpretations, yet you should allow the cards to help you discover your own deeper feelings and hidden thoughts. Enjoy the stories and let your imagination go on a wonderful journey!

The *Oracle of Mystical Moments* deck can be used in a daily routine, like having your special moment each day. I like to use the cards every morning. I pick one as a theme for the day. There are no strict rules to use the oracle deck. Just try and read it in a way you like best.

Begin by getting in a relaxed mood by listening to calm music, lighting a candle or preparing a hot cup of tea. Riffle the cards and lay the deck face down in front of you. Before picking a card, think about a question you have in mind or a certain mood you are in. Take a card and look at the story you see. Let your imagination and intuition wander. Before reading my explanation, think about your feelings while observing the card. There is no mystery behind it; it is your own subconscious speaking to you!

THE CARDS

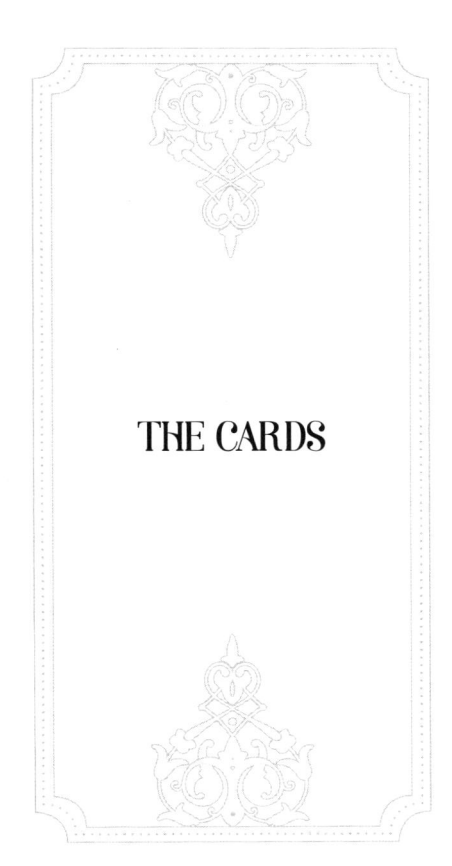

1. DAY & NIGHT

Uncertainty, Fear, Worries, Decisions to be made, Follow your instincts

The girl we see on this card is holding the sun in her hands while the moon is at her back. She looks uncertain, as if she has a question in mind but does not know the answer. What is she thinking about? Is she afraid of the answer or the inward process to find it? Many of us struggle with making decisions. But where there is shadow, there is also light. After a dark night there is always the light of the morning sun, warming the path we have chosen. This card reminds us that we already hold all the answers in our hands. We should trust our inner judgment and know we will be able to handle any situation.

2. LIBERTY

*Choices, Confidence, Letting go,
Self-determination*

This card shows a woman standing in profile. A birdcage hangs from her hair, and she is about to release her winged friend into the night. The stars and the moon are guiding the little bird's way. The woman has plucked a special star from the sky to help shepherd the bird's journey. This card stands for the freedom you have to choose your own way in life. Don't let others decide for you. You have the power to liberate yourself from both external and internal cages. Many of the obstacles we face are ones we create ourselves. Once we realize we've created them, we have the power to release them.

3. SLEEPING BEAUTY'S DREAM

Soul journey, Power of imagination, Inner strength

We all know the story of Sleeping Beauty, who got pricked by a spindle and fell into a deep sleep. This card shows Sleeping Beauty asleep, her hair thick like thorns surrounding a castle. Imagine if your soul could wander while you sleep. What places and people would it visit? Envision what kind of journey you could have. Your soul is not tied to a certain place. It is able to tear down walls and scale a hedge of thorns. Like the bird Sleeping Beauty gently holds in her hand, your soul is ready to be freed and soar to all the places in your dreams.

4. MOONDANCE

Daring, Balance, Easiness, Adventure, Perspective

Look at this girl balancing on a rope, waltzing with the moon. She is dancing through life! To be this confident is a gift you should be aware of and treasure. Be brave and adventurous. Get out of your comfort zone and see life from a different perspective. If you maintain a balance between levity and lightheartedness, you can stay above the everyday noise that threatens to bring us down. Feel the night breeze in your hair and adventure in your soul!

5. BLOOM

Self-confidence, Femininity, Individual fulfillment

A woman gazes into your eyes with pride and self-confidence. She knows what she wants, and this certainty blooms out of her being like a bountiful garden. Her hair is thick like the branches of trees, reaching out with controlled abandonment. The power of nature surrounds her, flowing both into her and out from her. What would it be like to feel this connected and confident? What could you accomplish? Your inner strength blossoms into future achievements.

6. LISTEN

Mindfulness, Sensitivity, Empathy

This young woman with closed eyes and a knowing smile is rooted in the earth. Her hair has transformed into the roots of the plants above her. You can tell the woman is aware of her surroundings. She is connected to the voice of nature. She can listen to the growing plants beneath the ground. She is an integral part of her world. She understands the sorrows and worries of the environment. She also knows the songs of nature's pleasures.

7. PURE NATURE

Grace, Blooming, Youth, Freshness

This young girl is flourishing as she develops into a woman. She loves her body and is aware of her unique beauty. Just as this girl does, cherish the beauty nature has given to you. See the softness and grace, and keep the secrets of youth in your heart! The red peony symbolizes respect and honor, ideals that must be recognized in ourselves before we can genuinely share our true nature with others.

8. RED GARDEN

Gratitude, Pleasure, Happiness

On this card we see a woman strolling through a garden full of flowers. The sky glows with pink petals and the ground has turned a luminescent blue. The woman finds great peace in being one with nature. The flowers have become part of her body and a parrot feels at home on her shoulder. During her walk down the path of life, she keeps happiness and gratitude in her heart. She notices the simple pleasure of life, and is thankful for all nature has given her.

9. ROSE GARDEN

Sensitivity, Awareness of nature, Integrated whole, Strength

Look at this beautiful woman who has transformed into a flower. She holds a red blooming rose to the place where her heart belongs. Her hair has become a leaf blown by the wind. She is a part of nature and grows stronger with her every gentle touch and loving gesture. She is not alone: her friends the caterpillar and butterfly are here to visit. Thorns threaten to prick her, but she is not scared. A rose is beautiful and strong because of its thorns, not in spite of them.

10. FLOWER SPIRIT

Friendship, Soul, Tenderness, Joy

This card shows the tender and sensitive flower fairy, the soul of each plant. She listens with all her heart to her friends, and provides a soothing caress when their edges get prickly. By enjoying life and keeping the playfulness in her heart, she is a source of inspiration and joy. Her childlike vision helps her see the good in all things, especially herself.

11. QUEEN BEE

Strength, Growth, Motherhood

Madam Queen Bee is big and strong, yet gentle and mothering. Her skirt is a flower tower, a home for bees that sustain our ecosystem. She gives strength, power and life to her surroundings. She is Mother Nature. She is responsible for the tulips that send energy into the world, and all that grows to know the beauty of each day. Her children are the children of earth. She nurtures all of us.

12. ALL IS CONNECTED

Innovation, Transformation, Growth, Release

A girl sits on a tree trunk and holds leaves in her hands, while others blow away in the wind. A small spider holds a few leaves together with his fine filament, even though the wind threatens to tear them apart. Don't be afraid of changes; release your fear by letting go. Change is hard and often painful, but it is the only way to grow. You may drift but you will never lose yourself. Life goes on and nothing ends, it is reshaped into something new by the wind. Not better or worse, but different, and in that change lies wonder and openings.

13. MORNING DEW GIRL

Face your fears, Awareness, Consciousness

The woman on this card collects fat raindrops into a basket of leaves. She is called "Morning Dew Girl", and she symbolizes the receiving and absorption of all worries and fears. She invites us to start sharing our own feelings and worries. We can collect them and deal with them instead of hiding them deep inside. She stands resolute and strong, ready to face her fears. While fear can be as powerful as a river, once confronted, it may turn out to be as small as a drop of dew.

14. THE ART OF SEDUCTION

Love, Womanhood, Passion, Seduction

We see an elegantly dressed couple; the woman close to the man as she whispers something in his ear. Is she talking about love? What kind of secrets is she telling him? In her red, jeweled gown, the woman is aware of her powers of seduction. She uses her femininity, beauty and passion. She tempts all of his senses, from the scent of a fragrant bloom to a soft touch on his check. There is incredible power in her gentle words and delicate caress.

15. ELIXIR OF LIFE

Healing, Consolidation, Reinvigoration, Truth

A woman is leaning towards a deep red rose. She faces the flower with her eyes closed, concentrating on the lush bloom. She is receiving the sweet scent of nature and the energy of life. The wind rustles her hair, whispering the truths of the universe into her ears. She can hear her own breath mingling with the wind. Sitting quietly in nature by a stream or in a garden can help still our wandering mind and heal a troubled heart.

16. EVA

Duplicity, Deception, Caution

Out of the jungle steps a woman, half of her body covered with exotic plants and flowers. A snake wriggles around her neck. The woman presents herself like a sweet fruit to be picked. She offers excitement and novelty, but be careful; her kiss could be as toxic as the bite of a snake. Like a deceitful friend or lover, her unreadable countenance masks her true intentions.

17. MISS SUNSHINE

Sun, Light, Energy, Courage, Clarity

A woman rises high into the sky. Her hair shines bright like the sun; her skirt looks like a huge building. She comes from a darker place, beneath her lies gloom and shadows. But her light is glowing. She is like the energy of life and the sun of the universe. She focuses her intentions on the positive and is able to gain clarity. She leaves the night and fears behind.

18. TREASURED MEMORIES

Memories, Nostalgia, Recognition

We see a woman sitting calmly in the grass. She looks forward to somewhere we don't know, while her mind is drifting in the past. With both hands she is holding a floating balloon filled with clouds. These clouds are old memories she wants to keep and treasure. Our past experiences don't define us—we can't live the life we had long ago. But the past does shape us, and remembrances of loved ones and joyful times can help us be our best selves today.

19. THE JOURNEY

Love of adventure, Curiosity, Appreciation

A young girl gently rides a deer. Both the girl and the deer are having fun on their adventure. They are playful and curious. Sometimes we get so caught up in the destination, we forget to appreciate the journey. But if we neglect the little things on our path, like soft grass under our feet or the unconditional love of an animal, we are missing out on precious moments. A new friend or acquaintance with a different point of view can help us see things we may have overlooked.

20. UNDER MY UMBRELLA

Compassion, Care, Friendship, Protection

A man is perched on the back of a giant parrot. He is holding an umbrella, which keeps the bird dry from the rain. This man is happy to help. He does not fear climbing up the big bird or a possible nip from her sharp beak. He is optimistic that his small umbrella is good enough to protect the bird from the weather. He is a true friend, aware of the power of a helping touch or smile to brighten someone's day. In turn, he is rewarded with a burst of color in his own life.

21. TINY TRIUMPHS

Attitude, Belief, Power of perseverance

A big mouse dressed as a circus trainer is holding a small eagle. The situation is inverted: The predator is small and the prey is big. This card urges us to believe in ourselves. Don't ever think you're too small or too outmatched in a situation. Inner size is what matters. Think back to a time when you felt good about an achievement. Don't give up now; with patience and hard work you will triumph in the end.

22. LIKE A BIRD

Focus, Forward looking, Possibilities, Motivation

A woman full of expectations looks into the future. There are no boundaries to what she can accomplish. Like the bird next to her who flies strong and direct, she knows now is the time for focused energy. You may have found yourself losing motivation lately, or questioning your decisions. The key to recapturing your passion lies in readjusting your focus to unlock creativity. Surround yourself with activities or people who make you feel inspired. They can be the breath of wind under your wings.

23. THE GIFT

Whimsy, Excitement, Curiosity, Gift

Under a snowy sky, a woman with feathered hair holds a little box. What is inside the box? We don't know for sure, but it seems to be a gift. Simple on the outside, but perhaps magical within. We can only imagine what would happen if we could tug the string and peer inside. Would it be the fulfillment of an old wish? Remember the curiosity we have before opening presents, the magical space between dreams and truth. A gift reminds us of the excitement we have in these special moments.

24. MERMAID'S LOVE

Love, Partnership, Support, Accord

A loving couple is shown on this card. The woman is a mermaid—her hair and tail seem to float her through the sky. A man with feathers holds her hand. He grounds and protects her; he is her base.

They are from different worlds, water and the sky, but they are complete together, a perfect love union. Their differences make them stronger and balanced. They support each other in their own way, but always from a place of respect and love.

25. PROTECTIVE NEST

Nurture, Motherhood, Protector, Incubation

Belying her serene expression, this woman is hatching more than just creative thoughts. She is a mother, creator of all. The giant bird's nest on her head holds three eggs and an older bird, already born into the world. Under her skirt, there is a glimpse of a large egg. This card symbolizes motherhood, protection of children, and how children develop under a mother's care. Be aware of how your actions or words can affect a fledgling soul.

26. TRANSFORMATION

Process, Identity, Seek answers

A woman is dressed in a red polka dot dress. The upper part has already begun the process of transforming into a butterfly. With her hand she touches her chest. Is the butterfly a part of her body? Is it a symbol of her soul? Is the woman transforming into a new life? This card leaves us with more questions than answers. Maybe you will find answers by thinking about how you would respond to these questions: Am I the person I would like to be? What can I do right now to transform some small part of myself?

27. THE GARDENER

Non-judgment, Acceptance, Self-compassion

Standing proud in a lush, green garden, a woman holds a growing bulb in her arms. Two small houses spring from the plant, and her skirt is transformed into a house.

She is the gardener of her soul, the caretaker of her home. Her feelings are the flowers of her garden. By taking care of herself, she keeps growing stronger. But sometimes uninvited guests invade the garden, intruders like jealousy or shame. If we recognize these as neither good nor bad, but something to be investigated and accepted, we can treat ourselves with compassion and keep blooming.

28. CAN YOU HEAR ME?

Loneliness, Cry for help, Communication

A woman floats in a seashell on the big sea. She looks to the horizon, as if she is waiting for somebody. She is holding a trumpet in her hand, ready to blow it when the time comes. The ocean symbolizes her feelings. Vast and seemingly unknowable, it surrounds her in an endless arc. She looks lonely and deserted. But she has a way of connecting, a tool for turning passive silence into supportive communication.

She just needs to raise her trumpet and call for help.

29. THE PERFECT KEY

*Happiness, Encouragement,
Unlock feelings*

This card shows a woman holding a key in one hand, and a cage with a heart in it in the other. There is a bird sitting on the woman's shoulder, encouraging her to try different keys with his mouth. Yet, the woman has already found the perfect-fitting key. She can open the cage and open her heart. Sometimes life is only a search for the right key. There are so many things that are hard for us to approach. We can have trouble accessing our own feelings. Thanks to friends and family, there are people who can help us find the lost keys to our personal happiness.

30. WHITE ROSE OF HOPE

Hope, Beacon, Solution, Beginnings

We see a woman dressed in a blue gown standing somewhere in a lonely landscape. Darkness surrounds her, but a shining white rose glows like a beacon and illuminates the night. Maybe this woman is lost, maybe she is uncertain about her feelings. Yet thanks to the light of the flower she can find her way. White roses symbolize hope, new beginnings, admiration and young love. There are exciting times ahead!

31. LORELEI

Power, Responsibility, Fate, Grace

A mermaid sits on a rock and gazes toward the ocean. A small ship floats nearby, connected with her through a rope. She has the power to decide the destiny of this ship and the fate of the crew. With a flick of her wrist, she could toss the ship against the shore, or she could let it continue its journey. What will the mermaid decide to do? She has suffered great loss in her own life. Will she continue the cycle of pain, or will she allow healing and grace to calm the waters?

32. TOUCH THE SKY

Lost in thoughts, Isolation, Sanctuary

A young girl with long braids looks down to earth from up in the skies. The small bird on her shoulder keeps her company in her cloud sanctuary. She is holding one of her braids like a lifeline, as if she is expecting somebody to climb up to her. Sometimes we are so overwhelmed by our feelings and sensations, we escape into a condition of withdrawal and separation. It is hard for other people to follow us there unless we give them a sign that they are welcome.

33. WEAVING FLOWERS

Creator, Art of the Universe, Integration

Here we see a woman gathering the delicate petals of blossoms and making them into flowers. It seems like she is weaving them together, bringing a greater whole into being. She is calm and concentrated on her work. This woman is a creator. She draws from the petals falling from the sky and growing from earth. Inspiration is all around. Gather it up to create a new whole.

34. ABRACADABRA

Magic, Secrets, Patterns, Destiny

Rising from a kingdom of skyscrapers, a giant woman glows in the cityscape. She is so tall she can touch the stars all around her. With her magic wand, she coaxes the future from the constellations. There is such order in the universe, in the golden ratio of a nautilus shell or patterns in the starry night. We can unlock the secrets of the universe. We are all the magicians of our own lives.

35. A LONG WAY HOME

Journey, Remembrances, Experiences, Passage

Look at this little elephant on his journey through the skies. He lives in a huge balloon and has his castle with him. Lights guide the way while he slowly passes over the horizon. How long is his journey and when will it end? Will he drop anchor again or continue his travels? This card reflects how we pass through our lives. During our pilgrimage we collect memories, strong enough to fill a castle and light enough to buoy our voyage.

36. HOUSE OF FLOWERS

Power of nature, Joy of life, Diversity, Beauty

Out of this small, white house on the top of a hill bursts flowers, full of life and rich in colors. It is like an explosion! The two ladies walking by look tiny in comparison to the giant, falling leaves. They enjoy the enormity of nature, the power of its diversity. But even a single bloom in a vase can transform a space, each petal a world unto itself and a wonder of creation. This card signals love for life in this moment full of energy, beauty and joy.

37. NO RAIN TODAY

Comfort, Positive view of life, Energy, Shine

In this card we see the sun banishing a crying cloud. There will be no rain today! The sun gives warmth and comfort. Her rays grant life and strength, they chase away grief and loss. On dark days, turn your face toward the sun and let the shadows fall behind you. Slip on your dancing shoes, if only for a moment, and let the energy move through your body. Surround yourself with positive, happy people to foster an environment where you can shine.

38. LULLABY

Restoration, Dreams, Rhythms, Lullaby

As dusk arrives, we notice a cello player about to play a lullaby, to welcome the sleep we need so dearly. The cycles of day and night, light and dark, orchestrate our natural sleep rhythms. We give so much during the day; night is our time to recover. On his instrument, we can see the moon and stars—they are the guardians of our dreams tonight. Rest with nature's lullaby blowing gently through the window. Tomorrow, wake to all the days of your life.

39. MY HOME IS MY CASTLE

Experience of Life, Growth, Knowledge, Age

The woman on the card carries a big castle on her shoulders. The castle is solid, it seems like it was growing each year of her life. The castle stands for the woman's soul. Inside its enduring walls, she keeps all her memories, thoughts, knowledge and feelings. The older the woman gets, the more this fortress of life grows. It keeps her company, defends her against pain, and provides the foundation for her true self to continue its journey.

40. OH SUNNY DAY

New beginnings, Luck, Optimism

A woman with a dainty umbrella sits on a red mushroom and watches the sun rise over the horizon. How nice it is to welcome a new day, especially with three little talismans of good luck—the ladybug. Embrace new beginnings; let us forget yesterday's worries and regrets. Don't allow the past to linger into today; all the moments in this day are brand new, never seen before or since. You have the power to make good things happen, you can make today your lucky day.

41. HOME IN THE SKY

Wanderlust, Adventure, Safe haven

Up in the sky we see a floating neighborhood of houses carried by balloons. Birds peek out through the windows. In this card there are elements of a journey, symbolized by the sky, birds and balloons. But there are also houses, which suggest home, security and stability. These birds have the best of both worlds—they can travel a big distance without losing their home. They are free to seek new experiences without worry. Home truly is where your heart is.

42. CHANGE OF SEASONS

Transformation, Life's ups and downs, Development

In the center of this card stands a woman surrounded by blowing leaves, flowers and snowflakes. As the wind blows them swirling up to her, she raises an arm in protection or welcome. We are not sure. This card reminds us that seasons change, just as we do. Nothing is ever still, not a river, not even the mighty oak, and certainly not us. We are in a constant state of transformation. Even when we feel overwhelmed, if we can just quietly be, we will be moving in spite of our ourselves. When life whirls around us, let the certainty of the cycle of seasons be a grounding force.

43. SECRETS

Magic, Mystery, Hidden thoughts

A girl on a stool is tall enough to reach the moon. She holds a ring of keys in her hand; one of them will fit in the keyhole on the moon's surface. This card tells us about personal secrets, hidden thoughts and ideas one keeps in their mind. Nobody is able to look inside your head unless you invite them to. You have the power to decide how much of your thoughts you want to share with others. A little mystery helps keep the magic alive.

44. STRANDED

*Misdirection, Misjudgment,
Fear of failure*

Look at this young sailor stranded with his ship on top of a tall tree. He needs his anchor to help him get back down to earth. The card asks: How did the ship get there? This is such an unusual place for a seafaring vessel! At times we feel the same; we find ourselves in situations we can't quite understand. Sometimes we feel we've made mistakes because our expectations are so high, we set ourselves up for failure. We either beat ourselves up over our performance, or we are so intimidated that we never even begin. Failure is a necessary part of success, as important to the journey as a rudder on a ship.

45. NEW DIRECTIONS

Departure, New perspectives, Goodbyes

A dandelion is an airship traveling through the sky with a top hat as the basket these men are flying away in. One man jumps out of the basket and sails off on a flying dandelion seed. It takes him far away, while the other men wave goodbye and wish him well. This story illustrates endings and departures that are necessary to gain new perspectives in life. It takes courage to change directions and abandon old habits. But if you are bold enough, you can fly toward something new—a dream, a place, even yourself.

46. NIGHT RIDE

Protector, Wonder in the night, Big brother, Friendship

An elephant transports two owls on his back, a mother with her young bird child. Protectively she has folded her wing over the young owl's head. The elephant rides through the night, blowing stars up into the sky through his trunk. Connected with magic and wonder, the elephant is a protector, a strong shoulder to lean on in all times. Even during dark times you can feel safe and secure beside him.

47. MY DEAR FRIEND

Lifelong friendship, Dependability, Solidarity

If you recall the card, "The Journey", you may recognize a similar scene here with a woman riding a deer. But this time both the woman and the deer are much older. Time has passed and the two are still companions. They have seen many seasons together, many sunny joys and cold sorrows. Their wisdom has grown, like the graceful antlers the woman holds for comfort. The deer supports her, and she returns a loving touch to her dear friend.

48. BUTTERFLY GARDEN

Curiosity, Discovery, Small moments in life

A woman holds a blooming flower in her hand as she gazes toward the sky. On her head sits a butterfly closely examining the purple petals. Enjoying the situation, the woman stands still and quietly soaks in her surroundings. She does not want to disturb the scene. In our daily life, there are so many possible moments that could be precious, if we would just take the time to notice them. Be mindful of your surroundings and pay attention. Ask, "Why is that there?" Then make connections. Small observations can lead to great discoveries.

49. KEYS ON TREES

Believe in yourself, Solutions, Creativity

On the top of a winding, shiny metal tower there is an elephant captured in a cage. A vast jungle of giant trees and plants surrounds him. But the elephant is not distressed. There are keys hanging from the trees, if he picks one he can open the cage and release himself into the wild. No situation is too complicated to be solved. Look in unexpected places for answers. You have the creativity to find the way out.

50. THE OBSERVER

Patience, Awareness, Focus

A woman is looking through an old fashioned camera, ready to take a photograph. She observes the landscape before her. All is quiet, all is peaceful. We don't know how long this woman has been waiting for the perfect shot.

She has the patience to remain focused until the decisive moment presents itself. Strength lies in her calmness. She lives in the present and does not get easily distracted.

51. TO THE MOON AND BACK

Desires, Wishes, Longings

Look at this woman sitting on a swing shaped like the moon. She gazes longingly into the distance, as if she would like to be somewhere else. Although her skirt is made out of feathers, she stays seated and does not fly away. This card speaks about strong desires. Sometimes we crave what we don't have. Instead of taking action, we remain passive and let our dreams fall unknown. Let the powerful magic of the moon reveal any unpredictable desires.

52. SEA WITCH

Innocence, Joy of play, Wonder

This small mermaid is called the "witch of the sea". Instead of a fishtail, she has a jellyfish on the lower part of her body. Her hair sways behind her like flowing tentacles. She holds a windmill in her hand that propels her forward. A wide-eyed fish is her loyal companion on her ocean journeys. She is young and uses the magic of childlike thinking to dance in the waves, marveling at the wonder of life.

ABOUT CATRIN WELZ-STEIN

In my art, I blur the lines between imagination and reality, while exploring womanhood in many different ways. I like to give my images a vintage, ethereal feel. During the creative process, I scan old paintings, photographs and illustrations, making sure they are in the public domain. I work digitally and transform the scans by first tearing them apart. They are like puzzle pieces that I work together, until they reveal a whole new meaning and tell an unknown story.

I started to create digital images when my children were two and four years old. At that time, I was desperate to do something creative. The images helped me to be aware of my feelings and worries. I did not plan to make them public; they were very personal, private images. Then I created Christmas cards and sent them to my family and friends. I was surprised by the positive reactions I got. After this encouragement, I became more courageous and started to post my images online. Now, I feel overwhelmed by all the positive feedback I have received! It is my motivation to go on with my work. I feel very blessed to be able to reach so many people's heart and souls.

Originally from Germany, I currently live with my family in Seoul, South Korea. We moved here in the summer of 2016, due to my husband's work. Previously, we lived in Kuala Lumpur, Malaysia. It is a blessing to be able to see so many parts of Asia. It has widened my horizons and I'm sure it also has influenced my artwork.

For our complete line of tarot decks, books, meditation cards, oracle sets, and other inspirational products please visit our website:

www.usgamesinc.com

U.S. Games Systems, Inc.
179 Ludlow Street
Stamford, CT 06902 USA
203-353-8400
Order Desk 800-544-2637
FAX 203-353-8431